Original title:
Tales Told Under Tall Trees

Copyright © 2025 Creative Arts Management OÜ
All rights reserved.

Author: Rosalie Bradford
ISBN HARDBACK: 978-1-80567-457-3
ISBN PAPERBACK: 978-1-80567-756-7

Hands of Time Among the Twisting Roots

Time flies by with a funny twist,
As squirrels practice their acrobat's list.
The owl hoots jokes, and the raccoons laugh,
While beavers measure wood with a silly graph.

The shadows dance as the sun goes down,
The fox pranks friends, running round and round.
A turtle tells tales in a slow, smart way,
While ladybugs gossip, just passing the day.

Chorus of the Canopy's Heart

The birds form a band in the leafy green,
With chirps and squawks, they're quite the scene.
A crow on a branch starts a comedy show,
And the trees sway gently, dancing to the flow.

The sun beams down, igniting their play,
As butterflies flutter, bringing bright ballet.
Laughter echoes through the branches high,
While acorns fall down with a soft, gentle sigh.

Whims of the Woodland Wanderers

Wanderers roam in a curious glee,
With mushrooms as hats and trunks as a 'tee'.
The chipmunks debate the fluffiest seat,
While rabbits plot mischief that can't be beat.

A deer plays tag with a group of fast mice,
While fireflies twinkle like stars in a dice.
Every leaf waves 'hello' with flair and fun,
In the magical woods where laughter's begun.

Reflections on the Forest's Edge

At the water's edge, the frogs hold court,
Croaking their humor in a lively sport.
A fish jumps up, giving a splashy cheer,
While turtles tell secrets, oh so sincere.

The wind sings softly, teasing the grass,
As critters line up for a grand, silly pass.
Under the stars, they share a great feast,
With giggles and chuckles, it's fun, to say the least.

Musings Beneath the Arched Canopy

Squirrels chatter with glee,
Their acorns rolled, oh what a spree.
A raccoon stole a picnic plate,
Now he dines on lunch—how great!

Laughter echoes through the leaves,
As children play, the sun weaves.
A bird dives down, a hat in sight,
It's just a game, a silly flight!

Time Stilled in the Timbered Vale

A turtle slowly struts his pace,
While crickets jump from place to place.
What a game of hide and seek,
With frogs that croak and mice that squeak!

The old oak whispers secrets near,
To passersby, they grin and cheer.
A squirrel juggles with his hands,
Gifts of nature, funny plans.

Songbirds and the Silent Stands

Chirping tunes, a feathery choir,
While butterflies dance, oh what a flyer!
A wise owl's snooze, a little tease,
He wakes up late—just lost the breeze!

Beneath the branches, shadows play,
An ant parade marches each day.
They tiptoe past, in suits of black,
While beetles roll balls, dancing back!

Under the Watchful Eye of the Elder

A wise tree chuckles at the scene,
Beneath its boughs, all's light and keen.
Kids tell jokes, their voices bright,
As twilight falls, a jovial sight!

Rabbits hop with mischief in mind,
Playing hide-and-seek with time aligned.
The elder chuckles, roots stretched long,
In this haven where we all belong.

The Parables of the Pines

In the shade where the squirrels convene,
A raccoon tells jokes that are quite obscene.
The branches sway, they giggle and creak,
The laughter so loud, it could make one weak.

A wise owl hoots from his leafy high throne,
He claims that the acorns possess minds of their own.
But when they roll off, oh, what a sight!
Their bouncing and tumbling brings joy to the night.

The chipmunks compete in a nut-gobbling race,
With their cheeks puffed out, what a comical space!
But when one trips, oh, they all swirl around,
In a flurry of giggles, they tumble to ground.

The wind whispers secrets, so silly and spry,
As the trees chuckle softly while watching the sky.
With creatures all laughing, the forest feels bright,
In this merry haven, they share pure delight.

Echoes of the Leafy Legends

In a grove where giggles dwell,
A squirrel tried to sing so well.
But the birds just rolled their eyes,
As he danced with clumsy sighs.

The wise old owl gave a wink,
While the raccoons made a stink.
'He's no Star,' the fox will chortle,
As they watched him splash in the portal.

Stories Woven in Bark

The tree stump hosted a debate,
On whether bugs could dance or skate.
They wiggled, jiggled, oh what a sight,
As the ants cheered them on with delight.

A snail challenged a beetle to race,
But it turned into quite a chase.
With laughter echoing through the glen,
The beetle lost—well, maybe again!

The Chronicles of Mossy Roots

Among the roots, a turtle sighed,
Dreaming of the world outside.
'Why run fast?' the rabbit chortled,
As he hopped and glided, almost startled.

A lizard on a log cracked jokes,
While nearby stood a group of folks.
'Why did the mushroom chase the sun?
Because it thought it could have some fun!'

Fables from the Forest Floor

The hedgehog threw a wild ball,
But hit a toadstool with a squall.
The mushrooms giggled, 'What a fall!'
As he rolled and landed with a sprawl.

A bumblebee hummed a tune,
While the flowers danced in June.
'Let's make a garden fit for kings,
With laughter as our offering!'

Folklore of the Forest Floor

A squirrel stole my sandwich, oh what a sight,
He danced on the branches, his grin pure delight.
The mushrooms giggled, sprouting upside down,
While rabbits held a party, wearing their best gowns.

The owls played poker, with acorns to bet,
And the fox made a fortune that no one could have met.
They swapped funny stories of a time gone by,
As leaves rustled softly, beneath the blue sky.

Heartstrings in the Heartwood

A woodpecker knocked on a tree's hollow chest,
To a beat that made critters tap dance and rest.
The beavers held hands, quite snug by the lake,
While the turtles all cheered for the jokes they could make.

A wise old owl hooted, "Who doesn't like pie?"
As butterflies giggled, flapping by high.
The night creatures whispered, 'We're all here for fun',
While shadows cast laughter—under moonlight they run.

Enigmas of the Emerald Grove

One raccoon wore glasses, had books piled high,
He pondered the stars with a curious eye.
The lizards debated if spots make them sleek,
While crickets all tuned up for a comical squeak.

The hedgehogs held races, but they just rolled slow,
With a finish line marked by a bright daisy glow.
They laughed at the nonsense, the fun without rules,
For every odd moment, they cherished the fools.

Myths Woven Through Wandering Roots

A cat with a hat claimed to speak for the trees,
He whispered sweet secrets carried by the breeze.
The ants held a festival, marching in line,
While fireflies twinkled, "Come dance and dine!"

Amidst all the laughter, a fox spun a tale,
Of a snail that dreamed big, but always turned pale.
Underneath the branches, their giggles took flight,
As the forest spun stories, wrapped in soft light.

Sunlight and Shade's Serenade

In the park where squirrels play,
Sunlight dances, chasing gray.
A rabbit hops with ease and grace,
While shadows tickle each lost trace.

The benches creak with tales so sly,
As lazy bees buzz gently by.
A squirrel snickers, plants a seed,
While wise old owls nod, take heed.

With laughter echoing in the light,
Each moment's sparkle feels just right.
Oh, how the world can spin and sway,
In this bright ballet of the day!

But watch your sandwich, don't forget,
The crafty critters are a threat.
In sunlight's glow, shade's laughter blooms,
A feast awaits, but not for you, I presume!

Dialogue Among the Dancing Leaves

Leaves gossip like old friends so dear,
Chattering secrets, full of cheer.
They twirl and twist beneath the breeze,
Sharing giggles, speaking with ease.

A crow squawks out the latest scoop,
While fireflies join in the group.
The branches sway, a gentle song,
Nature's whispers where all belong.

A gust comes by, they start to shout,
"What was that? Let's clear this doubt!"
With every rustle, tales unfold,
Of acorns lost and dreams retold.

Their laughter sways with every breeze,
In this grand dance among the trees.
Oh, how they prance, a sight to behold,
Such silly things, they never grow old!

Mysteries Beneath the Birdsong

A robin chirps a riddle bright,
While crickets hop, avoid the light.
In the underbrush, whispers flow,
Of secret treasures hidden low.

"Did you see the gopher's hat?"
"Or hear about the chubby cat?"
The sparrows share their wildest dreams,
As sunlight weaves through leafy seams.

With every note, a story's spun,
Of mischief, friendships, lots of fun.
Each feathered friend a sleuth by trade,
In this wacky world, they aren't afraid.

So join the chorus, sing along,
With chirps and caws, you can't go wrong.
For in this chatter, joy is found,
In playful secrets, life's profound!

A Constellation of Leaves

Underneath the leafy skies,
Stars are born, and laughter flies.
A dandelion wishes, makes a scene,
While whispers spin like a bright vaccine.

The oak will joke, "I'm older still!"
While maples shrug on their brown frill.
"Who's the funniest of the grove?"
Laughter bubbles, a fickle trove.

With a rustle here, a giggle there,
Each branch holds secrets, mischievous flair.
They tell of squirrels with a playful leap,
And owls who snore instead of keep.

As shadows stretch and day turns night,
The leaves converse, bask in delight.
Oh, what a show these trees can weave,
A constellation born from the eve!

Whispers in the Canopy

Squirrels chatter, plotting mischief,
Acorns fall like tiny bombs,
Leaves giggle in the rustling air,
As woodpeckers drum joyful songs.

Chipmunks dance, their tails like feathers,
Drawn to the rhythm of the breeze,
The sun peeks in, a curious fellow,
Shining bright through swaying trees.

A raccoon's mask in shadowed laughter,
Stealing snacks from picnicking friends,
Beneath the giggles, nature's chatter,
The woodland's humor never ends.

In this tall arena, stories thrive,
With every branch a joke retold,
Nature's comedy will survive,
In the canopy, brave and bold.

Secrets of the Elderwood

In the shade where the wise ones gather,
Old tales bloom like wildflowers,
A fox in glasses, quite the chatter,
Reciting poems for hours and hours.

The wise old owl, a jester at heart,
Makes puns that echo through the glade,
While butterflies waltz, a colorful art,
Colors bright beneath the shade.

Rabbits wearing hats, a fancy affair,
Debating which cloud looks like cheese,
Amidst the giggles, laughter to share,
Even the trees bend with ease.

From roots to crowns, the jesters play,
Creating worlds of whimsy and fun,
In the elderwood, they dance all day,
Under the warm and golden sun.

Shadows of the Ancient Grove

Whispers echo in the evening breeze,
Where shadows play and giggle light,
A turtle in shades, quite the tease,
Trying to catch fireflies at night.

Laughter weaves through ancient trunks,
From critters hiding in the dark,
Each rustle brings chuckles and flunks,
In this grove, there's always a spark.

Badgers wearing capes, quite a sight,
Hosting shows with their stolen meals,
Every joke under the moon so bright,
Turns the night into spinning wheels.

In the cozy twilight, stories unfurl,
From acorn pies to nutty stews,
Beneath a canopy, laughter will swirl,
In this grove, amusing views.

Beneath the Arboreal Whisper

Under branches swaying and swishing,
Creatures gather by the brook,
Rabbits conjuring caramel fishing,
With tales hidden in every nook.

The fox wears a crown made of twigs,
Declaring himself the King of the Wood,
While owls hoot jokes, everyone digs,
In a realm where all things are good.

Fireflies flash, a disco delight,
As frogs croak rhythms that shine,
Nature's party stays up all night,
With every wink, they sip on sunshine.

In this woodland, humor runs free,
With echoes of laughter timelessly spun,
Underneath each wise, stately tree,
Life's laughter is never done.

The Saga of the Silent Saplings

In the wood, a squirrel danced,
While the trees just stood and pranced.
They whispered quips, a secret joke,
As acorns dropped with every poke.

A chipmunk grinned with tiny hands,
Championed by his nutty bands.
"Why don't you laugh?" the branches plead,
But the trunks just shrugged, "We don't have speed!"

The owls winked, their eyes so bright,
"Join the fun, let's take flight!"
But grounded roots would never budge,
Staying planted, that was their grudge.

So the forest echoed with chuckled cheer,
While saplings giggled, not a soul to fear.
Though still as stones, beneath skies so blue,
In the heart of the woods, joy grew anew.

Under the Shade of Tall Sentinels

Beneath the giants, a gathering roar,
Frogs in bow ties croaked tales of yore.
With twigs for wands, they waved with glee,
Proclaiming themselves the lords of spree.

A bumblebee buzzed, wearing a crown,
While ants paraded, never a frown.
"Join us for snacks!" the ladybugs sang,
With cookies made from berries they sprang.

The tall pines chuckled, their needles a-shake,
As the rabbit brigade made a grand mistake.
They tried to dance but stumbled on roots,
Falling all over, in furry, lost suits!

Yet laughter chimed like a sweet serenade,
Echoing brightly in sunlight's parade.
The shade held secrets, and stories so grand,
Under the sentinels, joy took a stand!

Myths Carved in the Ages

In the old grove, vines held a plot,
Of heroes who battled, or so they thought.
A mouse in armor took off with a prize,
While the oak just chuckled, rolling its eyes.

Squirrels held court, their tails like a flag,
Flinging acorns as warriors brag.
Around them, shadows danced on the floor,
As the moonlight giggled, wanting more.

Every crack in the bark told a fib,
Of a dragon who sneezed, causing a rib.
Yet who would believe in such fanciful tales,
When the trees held secrets beneath their veils?

But laughter rippled through every leaf,
For the forest knew joy was the true belief.
Carved in its spirit, beneath skies ablaze,
Are myths made to lighten the hardest of days.

The Enchanted Glade's Memoirs

In a glade where shadows play hide and seek,
A raccoon told stories — quirky, unique.
With his bandit mask and clever refrain,
He spun tales where the bizarre was plain.

A turtle raced, or pretended to fly,
While the birds couldn't help but giggle nearby.
"Life's just a game! Come join the fun!"
They chirped and they cheered, under the sun.

The flowers joined in, with colors bright,
Tickling each other, pure delight.
And with every flutter, petals burst free,
Dancing in rhythm, as joyous as can be.

In the enchanted glade, the laughter bloomed,
While nature's critters all joyously zoomed.
With memories made in every soft breeze,
The glade held its magic, as sweet as the trees.

Reflective Ripples in Rooted Remembrance

Beneath the branches wide and grand,
We gather stories, hand in hand.
Squirrels gossip, leaves all giggle,
While ants in line pose and wiggle.

With acorns dropped, we share our dreams,
A raccoon in stars, or so it seems.
Laughter echoes through the green,
As laughter makes the forest keen.

The breeze it whispers, secrets old,
Of epic feats and mischief bold.
We reminisce of silly fights,
And dance till close of sunny nights.

So come, oh friends, let's play our game,
Forget the world, forget the shame.
For every laugh, a tree will grow,
In this funny show, the roots will glow.

The Celestial Canopy

Under the expanse of leafy embrace,
We chuckle and nudge in a playful space.
A crow cracks jokes we can't quite catch,
As shadows shift, and branches scratch.

Pine cones reign as royal crowns,
While fireflies wear their light-up gowns.
We spin old yarns of silly pranks,
A frog in trousers, and a raccoon who thanks!

The sun peeks through with a playful grin,
As we laugh loud enough to wake a bear's kin.
Each rustling leaf holds a secret queer,
In this canopy, we shed every fear.

So gather round, let's weave our fun,
As pine and cedar dance in the sun.
The stories sprout from roots so wide,
In laughter's light, we all abide.

Phantoms of the Fern-Flecked Silence

In whispers soft where ferns do sway,
Ghostly giggles hover and play.
Beneath the fronds, we poke and tease,
Casting shadows like the autumn breeze.

A phantom cat takes a silly leap,
While owls and crickets pretend to sleep.
We tread on laughter, soft as air,
With silly stories to share with flair.

As shadows dance on the forest floor,
A deer swings by, then ducks for more.
We recount times we slipped and fell,
In this fern-flecked spell where laughter dwells.

So come and join this ghostly jest,
Where humor reigns and hearts are blessed.
In the silent giggles, we find our place,
Among the ferns, a timeless grace.

Journeys in the Shade of Giants

Beneath the giants, we roam so free,
With silly maps and cups of tea.
We embark on quests for treasure rare,
Only to find it's just fresh air.

Each bark holds tales of snickers and cheer,
While mushrooms gossip, lending an ear.
We dodge the twigs as we run, sprint, leap,
With wild banter that even squirrels keep.

In mossy crannies we make our throne,
Where giggles grow on roots we've sown.
Fairies chuckle, playing tricks with glee,
In the shade where we're all wild and free.

So raise your cups, let's toast to fun,
To playful hearts, and the big, warm sun.
For in this forest where time stands still,
Each laugh is a journey up a hill.

Green Dreams of the Tranquil Thicket

In a thicket green as a pickle,
Whispers dance like a silly tickle.
Squirrels plot with acorn capes,
Frogs croak jokes, wearing leafy drapes.

Breezes giggle in the dappled light,
As chipmunks stage a wobbly fight.
The trees lean in, their branches sway,
Echoing laughter of the playful day.

Beneath a bush, a rabbit prances,
Tripping over his own funny chances.
With every hop, he shows his flair,
While hedgehogs chuckle, rolling everywhere.

In this vibrant patch of delight,
Where mischief hides from morning's light,
The woodland critters know their theme:
Life is better when you laugh and dream.

Shadows of the Storytellers' Hollow

In the hollow where the shadows play,
An owl hoots jokes in a quirky way.
The raccoons gather with hats so tall,
Trading puns 'neath the elder's sprawl.

A fox spins tales of bold escapes,
While trees nod gently, their trunks in capes.
The bunnies giggle at each funny twist,
In the light of the moon, who could resist?

Grasshoppers join with a tap-tap sound,
As crickets chirp, spinning tales profound.
The characters strut in an ensemble cast,
Creating laughter that echoes vast.

In this hollow where the sunlight creeps,
Funny stories are what the forest keeps.
With every shadow and subtle grin,
The magic is real, let the fun begin!

Moonbeams and Woodsy Whispers

Under moonbeams soft as cream,
A bear hums his favorite theme.
Badgers nod with sleepy eyes,
As the night air bursts with silly sighs.

The owls converse in riddles bright,
While fireflies join the playful fight.
Each flicker shows a winking prank,
The glow of laughter fills the bank.

Squirrels dance on branches light,
Telling stories that fill the night.
They leap and twirl, quite carefree,
As shadows twist in harmony.

In this world where whispers play,
The woods are bursting with fun today.
Each laugh and giggle lifts the gloom,
In the heart of night, wild dreams bloom.

Reveries in the Ruins of Roots

In ancient roots where laughter stirs,
A raccoon whispers, "Have you heard?"
With every creak of the gnarled wood,
The stories twist as they surely would.

A crow caws jokes from way up high,
As rabbits bounce with a gleeful sigh.
The ivy leans in to catch a bit,
Of the teasing words that never quit.

In the ruins where the jesters play,
Old trees stretch in a sprightly way.
Each leaf flutters in a playful game,
As critters run wild, not caring for fame.

In this magic where the roots entwine,
Stories blossom, weird and fine.
With every grin and funny wink,
Nature chuckles, making us think.

Revelations in the Rustling Leaves

The squirrels debate who's the best,
One thinks it's all in the nutty jest.
The woodpecker laughs from his lofty post,
Claiming he's surely the feathered host.

A rabbit rolls in a patch of grass,
Dares the badger to join him, alas!
With each silly hop, they start to race,
As the owls hoot, it's a funny chase.

A raccoon swipes snacks from the campfire,
While a chipmunk exclaims, "That's not my desire!"
Each critter giggles at the mayhem made,
In the evening light, their worries fade.

Under the glow of a setting sun,
Every creature feels the joy, oh fun!
With laughter echoing through the green,
The forest awakens, a playful scene.

Chronicles from the Heart of the Woods

In shadows deep where the branches twist,
A frog on a log cannot be missed.
He croaks of the flies that flew the coop,
While a bounding deer joins the giddy group.

A turtle dreams of a marathon race,
Though moving slow, he speeds up the pace.
The rabbits giggle, "He'll never win,"
As the trees chuckle at the woodland spin.

A fox plays tricks with a feathered fowl,
"Think you can dance?" he gives a sly howl.
But the hen clucks back, "Not so fast, my friend,
Your fancy footwork will meet its end!"

At dusk they gather in a grand old ring,
With stories of wise acorns and spring.
Each laugh a spark in the woodsy air,
Nature whispers joy, no room for despair.

Moonlit Meetings of the Old Oak

By moonlit glow, the night is alive,
Creatures hop out, all eager to jive.
A hedgehog rolls in a dance so bold,
While the wise old owl shares tales of old.

Two badgers conduct a silly debate,
"What's the best snack? You can share your plate!"
A wise rabbit throws in his crunchy two cents,
While the crickets chirp, their voices immense.

A raccoon dons a hat made of leaves,
Pretends to be king, and everyone heaves.
The woodlands echo with laughter so sweet,
As tree trunks sway to the rhythm of feet.

Those moonlit meetings under the boughs,
Bring joy and mischief, and cheeky vows.
In the embrace of night, they twirl and spin,
The magic of friendship, a dance to begin.

Beneath the Boughs of Memory

Under the boughs where giggles reside,
A fox and a crow take a joyride.
"Yo, let's play tricks!" says the cunning beast,
"On the farmer's dog, at the very least!"

With branches shaking, the laughter flows,
While a tortoise shares his foot-tapping prose.
"I may be slow, but let's count my cheer,
For every bad pun, there's a flash of deer!"

A lively squirrel starts a sing-along,
Each note uproarious, nothing feels wrong.
The moon above winks at their playful spree,
As shadows dance, young and free as can be.

Together they weave, a tapestry bright,
Beneath the old trees, their souls feel light.
With chuckles and whispers, the night slips away,
In the heart of the woods, where friendships play.

Songs of the Swaying Limbs

In the shade of branches wide,
Squirrels chatter, a silly guide.
One lost a nut, oh what a scene,
A dance so wobbly, yet so keen.

Birds gossip in loops so round,
Each feathered friend with jokes abound.
A frog in the pond joins the fun,
With a leap and a splash, he's number one!

Under the leaves, a picnic spread,
Ants in line, all hopes to be fed.
A sandwich lost, what a wild chase,
Nature laughs, at this nutty race!

As evening falls, we share a grin,
With whispers of laughter, the moment's win.
The breeze has secrets, all softly hum,
In this jolly grove, we're never glum.

Chronicle of the Canopy's Embrace

Once in a forest, a curious crow,
Thought he was king, putting on a show.
He landed on logs, with great delight,
But forgot how to land, oh what a sight!

The owls behind him giggled in glee,
While raccoons rolled, 'Come join, oh me!'
A dance-off sparked, who'd take the crown?
But the crow just tripped and tumbled down!

The trees whispered tales of the bold crow's fall,
With tales of goofiness, echoing tall.
Fallen leaves giggled, as breezes played,
In this circus of nature, all debts were paid!

When moonlight spilled, the laughter soared,
In the canopy's arms, silliness roared.
Mirth in the bark, joy in the breeze,
Together we'll laugh, under ancient trees.

Dreams Danced in the Rustling Leaves

In twilight's glow, the shadows prance,
A rabbit wearing shoes tries to dance.
With floppy ears, he leaps and twirls,
Bringing giggles from all the girls!

The fireflies blink like tiny stars,
While raccoons play drums on old jars.
A singing toad croaks a silly song,
As the moon joins in, humming along.

A wise old owl hoots, 'Oh what a sight!'
'Can you simply dance during the night?'
Our laughter echoed through the trees,
As squirrels joined in, with such great ease!

The stars peeked down with smiles so bright,
In this whimsical world of sheer delight.
So close your eyes and sway with the leave,
In a dance of dreams, there's nothing to grieve.

Echoes of Enchanted Evenings

As sunlight fades, dusk starts to play,
A parrot tells jokes in a cheeky way.
He squawks of pirates, treasure, and gold,
With punchlines so funny, we're never too old.

Rabbits hop over, eager to hear,
The tale of the parrot, squeaky and clear.
Caught up in laughter, they tumble and roll,
In this lively patch, humor takes a toll!

Owls serve drinks, with laughter and cheer,
With sips of dew and a splash of fear.
'Hold your hats!' the wise one will shout,
For the wind is a character, there's no doubt.

As night wraps around like a cozy quilt,
Bringing chuckles, not a hint of guilt.
With echoes of giggles, the stars above,
In this enchanted realm, we share the love.

The Enchanted Leaf Embers

Once a leaf dreamed of flight,
To escape from its branch at night.
It tickled a breeze with a giggle,
And danced like a kid doing a wiggle.

The moon chuckled, 'You silly green thing!'
'You're bound to that branch, like a puppet on string.'
But the leaf just laughed, wise beyond belief,
'At least I have fun, who needs a leaf sheath?'

The wind spun around, with a twist and a shout,
'Join me in a whirl, let's laugh and flout!'
They looped through the dark, in a spiral delight,
While squirrels peered out, thinking, 'What a sight!'

So remember the leaf, though its dreams may be small,
Always find joy, let your laughter enthrall.
For life's a grand show, with no reason to pout,
Just twirl with the wind, and let your joy sprout.

Conversations with the Whispering Pines

Under the pines, secrets they weave,
One joked to another, 'Do you believe?
That chipmunk over there thinks he's a star,
But look at him scurry, he's not going far!'

'Oh, hush!' said one, 'He's a pro at disguise,
In stripes and in shades, he's truly wise!'
'Then what about us? All trunks and no flair?'
The pine laughed aloud, 'Well, we've strength to share!'

As the breeze brushed by, they whispered and bragged,
Contests of tall tales, their bark lyrics tagged.
'Remember last spring, when we caught that parade?
Those ants wore tiny hats, they really displayed!'

So under those branches, jesters of wood,
The pines had a party, just like they could.
With laughter around, and nature's refrain,
Life's best conversations sprout joy in the grain.

The Sage of the Sylvan Glade

In a glade where the shadows like secrets would lie,
   Said a squirrel to a rabbit, 'Oh, peek at the sky!'
   'What wisdom you carry, old tree of the sage!
   Do you see how we frolic? Is it all just a stage?'

The sage, with his bark, chuckled deep with delight,
'Oh, young ones, keep dancing, you're perfect tonight!
   Life's a bit silly, just a game of charades,
   With acorns for laughter and twigs for parades.'

The rabbit donned glasses, a chips-and-dip feast,
'It's true, Mr. Sage, my thoughts feel increased!
But what's the best joke, oh wise one so grand?'
'How about the one about the cow in a band?'

So with jokes floating 'round, and giggles alight,
The sage watched them play till the day turned to night.
For wisdom is funny, when shared with good cheer,
   So laugh with the trees, and forget all your fear.

Dreamscapes Between the Limbs

High up the branches, a dream took its flight,
Over here, over there, it's a whimsical sight.
Two owls in glasses debated the day,
'Who stole my last snack? It was here—then away!'

One hooted in stray, a wisecrack to share,
'Maybe it danced off, wearing fine underwear!'
They chuckled together, the stars winked above,
And floated on clouds, like kids in love.

Then the moon joined the fun, with a giggle so bright,
'What's better—sneaking snacks or the thrill of a flight?'
They pondered the question, their laughter like streams,
Creating a night full of wild, wicked dreams.

So if you see owls, just know they're up there,
Finding joy in their tales, like magic to share.
In the laughter of nature, let your spirit roam free,
For the dreamscapes of limbs are where humor will be.

Tales of the Timberline Twilight

Beneath the branches, squirrels dance,
They steal our snacks, not a single chance.
The owls hoot jokes, a wisecrack cheers,
While we burst out laughing, despite our fears.

The shadows grow long, the moon starts to peek,
A raccoon pops out, with a grin on its cheek.
It flips a coin, and with luck, it flies,
Claiming the prize of the stars in our eyes.

The pinecones tumble like bowling balls,
The laughter echoes as twilight calls.
From tree to tree, we share our glee,
In this twilight realm, forever free.

As night unfurls, tales take their flight,
In the glow of fireflies, everything feels right.
With giggles and smiles, we'll recount the fun,
Under the watch of the toasty sun.

Hallowed Grounds of the Evergreen

The forest whispers secrets and cheers,
With playful echoes of ancient years.
A bear plays cards with a fox full of flair,
As we slip on roots, sliding with care.

The trees all chuckle, swaying and swaying,
A chipmunk juggles, and we start playing.
A breeze brings tales from the branches high,
With laughter bubbling like sap from the sky.

A mossy bank, our sit-and-tell time,
With frogs croaking rhythm, a fanciful rhyme.
Each giggle shared makes the shadows grow long,
In the heart of the pines, we just belt out a song.

Here stories blossom, wild and free,
Grinning like kids in an open spree.
With every chuckle, the night comes alive,
In hallowed grounds, together we thrive.

Starlit Stories from the Sycamore

Under the sycamore, we gather round,
With eyes all aglow and laughter profound.
A porcupine winks, and the crickets chime,
As we share our tales, we groove to the rhyme.

The owls are storytellers, wise and sly,
They spin wacky yarns that make us cry.
A raccoon bids on our campfire pizza,
With toppings of giggles and nights that are breezy.

The stars overhead twinkle in delight,
While shadows dance in the warm, sweet night.
Each tale we tell, with a twist and a tease,
Leaves us all rolling, hearts full of ease.

So let the stories under starlight glow,
With laughter resounding in the ebb and flow.
For here in the magic of this nightly spree,
We'll weave silly yarns, just you and me.

The Lingering Breath of the Great Oak

By the great oak, we sit and conspire,
Recalling the time of the silly flat tire.
With critters convening, they add to the show,
As the breeze rustles softly, like whispers below.

A woodpecker knocks, joining our spree,
While a goofy raccoon steals jelly from me.
The fungus giggles; a gnome gives a wink,
Every moment here makes me pause and think.

The stories flow like sap in the spring,
Of bug contests hosted and squirrels with bling.
Each chuckle we share gives the trees a sway,
As echoes of laughter refuse to decay.

So let's raise a toast with mugs full of cheer,
To the great oak's laughter, we hold so dear.
For under its branches, we'll always find,
The humor in life that leaves us entwined.

Moonlit Reveries Between Branches

In the glow of the moon so bright,
Raccoons dance, what a silly sight.
With each twirl and goofy glance,
They invite the owls to join their dance.

Squirrels gossip with a chuckle,
Tales of acorns and the big tree tussle.
A deer strolls by, with elegance so grand,
Wonders if the grass is better than the sand.

Fireflies flash like tiny stars,
While foxes claim they can run for miles far.
Each creature plays their part in jest,
Imitating frogs, they think they're the best.

As the night unfolds with a wink and a tease,
The tall trees sway, dancing with ease.
In this mirthful woodland, all is bright,
Laughter echoes under the soft moonlight.

Legends of the Woodland Watchers

Beneath the branches, whispers arise,
Squirrels spout nuggets of great surprise.
They wear tiny hats, what a sight to behold,
Swapping stories both silly and bold.

The wise old owl gives a knowing hoot,
Claims to have seen a dancing newt.
Frogs croak a tune, in a comical way,
Making the moonbeam have a laugh play.

Chipmunks wear shoes, racing up the hill,
Tripping on roots, they giggle and thrill.
A hedgehog joins in, with a swagger so cool,
Proclaiming himself as the woodland's best fool.

When twilight descends, and shadows do blend,
The chums tell their tales that never seem to end.
A symphony of laughs in the cool forest air,
Legends grow thicker, spreading joy everywhere.

Verses from the Verdant Depths

Underneath leaves, where secrets lie,
The raccoons plot with a crooked eye.
An acorn cap becomes a crown,
While leafy gowns make them dance around.

The owls share riddles, silly and neat,
What has wings but can't be beat?
A playful gust whirls stories around,
As giggles erupt from the soft ground.

A rabbit hops in, proud and spry,
Claiming he's the fastest, oh me, oh my!
The others roll on the grass in glee,
Challenging him under the old elm tree.

As shadows grow long, the fun carries on,
Under verdant boughs, till the break of dawn.
Every creature joins in the merry spree,
In this vibrant glen, they all feel free.

Narratives of the Timeless Trunks

Beneath the wise, old trunks so wide,
Lies a gathering, full of pride.
With roots like stories, thick and deep,
Rabbits share dreams they dare to keep.

Fireflies flicker, lighting up the scene,
As imaginative squirrels share what they've seen.
Fable of the wind, how it tickles the leaves,
Bringing delight that hardly deceives.

A porcupine grins, with quills all aflare,
Telling how he once dyed his hair.
Each chuckle of joy fills the gentle air,
Creating a magic, beyond compare.

When twilight falls, and the stars appear,
The trunks stand tall, ready to hear.
In the laughter and joy, not a worry in sight,
They celebrate friendship, through the still night.

Chronicles of the Whispering Wind

There once was a squirrel, a bit of a tease,
He'd steal all the acorns, with such silly ease.
The birds would all chirp, raising quite a ruckus,
While the poor grounded fox just felt quite the circus.

A turtle named Tim thought he'd give it a try,
To catch that sly squirrel, but oh, my oh my!
He sprinted on two legs; what a sight, oh so grand,
The squirrel just laughed, eating seeds from his hand.

The wise old owl watched with a roll of his eyes,
As the forest critters crafted their clever lies.
A contest was held, who'd bring the best joke,
The prize was a dance with the fat, giggling oak.

At dusk when they gathered, the fun was extreme,
With giggles and laughter, it felt like a dream.
The wind swirled around, whispering to all,
"Join in on the fun, don't forget to have a ball!"

Heartbeats of the Forest's Heart

In the depth of the woods, a party went wild,
The mushrooms were dancing, oh what a child!
The raccoons brought snacks in their little bandits' masks,
As laughter erupted from all sorts of tasks.

An owl played the drums, while a rabbit tapped feet,
The music was lively, oh, what a sweet beat!
The deer spun around with a twirl and a hop,
Until one lost a shoe, and fell with a plop.

"Who ordered the fox in a tutu so bright?"
Chirped the chatty bluebird, creating delight.
The hedgehogs were giggling, rolling around,
While everyone searched for the laugh-making sound.

As the moon glowed above, and the night wore thin,
They danced 'til the stars fell, grinning wide with a grin.
Each heartbeat of forest, echoing with cheer,
Proved life is more fun with friends gathered near.

The Lore of Lush Green Canopies

Underneath the canopy, whispers abound,
A chipmunk named Charlie was famed for his sound.
With jokes sharp as thistles, tickling the air,
He'd make all the animals laugh without care.

A tortoise named Tilly could tell quite a tale,
Of the time that the crow stole her snack without fail.
But clever was Charlie, he outsmarted the bird,
Swapping seeds for a whoop, oh, it was absurd!

The porcupines giggled, their quills all afluff,
As Tilly recounted each part of the stuff.
They held a big feast to share in the cheer,
With pies made of acorns—a treat, oh so dear!

As the sun dipped low, casting shadows so neat,
The animals rang out with their chorus of sweet.
With laughter still lingering, they pledged a great vow,
To gather again for more fun, here and how!

Imprints of Time in Timber

In a treeful of tales, stood a wise old oak,
With wisdom so vast, he'd balderdash and joke.
"Why did the pine tree never lose its mind?"
He'd grin with a twinkle, "It was hard to find!"

The birches would giggle, their trunks all a shiver,
As the oaks shared stories, a true timber river.
Of branches that danced and roots that would sway,
While nuts dropped like laughter, brightening the day.

A raccoon with goggles proclaimed himself grand,
"I'm the king of the nuts, if you lend me a hand!"
With a flick of his paw, he caused quite the cheer,
As the branches all echoed, "Let's do it right here!"

As twilight embraced the towering trees,
The chorus of critters joined in with the breeze.
With nightfall's embrace, laughter echoed the ground,
While the wisdom of woodlands thrived all around.

Legends Carved in Bark

Once a squirrel stole a nut,
A chatter started, oh what a strut!
He danced on branches, gave a shout,
As branches shook, the acorns fell out.

The owl winked, quite amused,
Said, "This nutty chap's quite confused!"
He hooted loud with a cheeky grin,
As the forest laughed at the squirrel's spin.

A hedgehog rolled with a lighted flair,
Dreaming of dancing in the cool night air.
He stumbled and tumbled, oh what a sight,
The forest erupted in giggles that night.

Every branch had a story to share,
As whispers floated high through the air.
So next time you roam where shadows play,
Remember the laughs of the woodland's day.

Fables of the Woodland Spirits

In the glen, where spirits sway,
A gnome named Fred fancied ballet.
He twirled and spun, much to their cheer,
Until he tripped on a deer's pet ear.

The fairies giggled, their wings aglow,
"More grace, dear Fred, just take it slow!"
With wobbly feet, he gave a grin,
And swept up leaves as he twirled again.

A funny fox joined the fray,
Said, "Let's have a contest, hooray!"
But as he pranced, he lost his tail,
Creating chaos; it was a wild tale.

At twilight's end, they all did rest,
No woodland creature could contest,
For laughter echoed among the trees,
Their nightly stories carried by the breeze.

The Moonlit Grove Chronicles

Under the moon, shadows played,
The raccoons plotted a grand charade.
"Let's steal berries from that vine!"
They snickered softly, their eyes did shine.

But owls were wise and sat on high,
Shook their heads with a knowing sigh.
The raccoons stumbled, covered in dirt,
As laughter erupted from a nearby bird.

A frog in the pond joined the fun,
Challenging the gang to a hopping run.
They bounced and croaked, what a sight!
Nighttime antics, pure delight.

When the dawn broke, they'd share the lore,
Of midnight mischief, oh, so much more.
With stories carried on the cool breeze,
These moonlit moments brought such ease.

Lullabies of the Tree Tops

High in the branches, a squirrel crooned,
A lullaby soft, the forest attuned.
An endearing tune drifted so sweet,
While bees buzzed softly, keeping the beat.

The rabbits gathered, quite in a stack,
To hear about adventures of the old knapsack.
With bouncing tales of a distant hill,
They laughed so loud, their hearts did fill.

A wise old turtle spoke with delight,
"Even slowpokes can take flight!"
The woodland critters, a rollicking crew,
Joined in laughter, for they all knew.

As stars began to twinkle bright,
The lullabies turned into cheers of light.
They held hands softly, swaying in time,
Under the moon, their spirits did climb.

Petals and Shadows

In the garden where daisies play,
A butterfly steals my lunch today.
With a giggle, it flits away,
While I laugh, oh what a dismay!

A squirrel joins in on the fun,
Juggling acorns, not quite done.
He slips and falls, oh what a run,
Chasing shadows, and then he's gone!

Nearby, a snail in a top hat,
Thinks he's the ruler, imagine that!
He struts with pride, but falls flat,
Turns to me and says, "Fancy that?"

Under blooms where laughter grows,
Petals dance with the punchlines close.
Nature whispers in gentle throes,
As we enjoy a comedy prose!

A Tapestry of Bark and Breeze

Beneath the branches, whispers sway,
A bird jokes, 'Who needs a toupee?'
A nut case squirrel, he's on display,
With his wild thoughts going astray.

The ancient oak with a wise old face,
Chuckles softly, keeping pace.
"Life's a race, but oh dear grace,
I've got the best seat in this place!"

The wind teases the leaves just right,
Spinning yarns till the stars ignite.
A tale unfolds in the moonlight,
Little critters dancing in delight.

Laughter lingers on the night's breeze,
Each chuckle carried by the trees.
In this place of fun and ease,
Life's a giggle wrapped in leaves!

Echoing Laughter in the Lush Landscape

On a hill where the daisies sing,
A frog jumps and lands like a spring.
He croaks a tune, a funny thing,
As the bugs around him start to cling.

A rabbit hops with a wiggly nose,
Telling tales in his polka-dotted clothes.
With each leap, their humor grows,
While sunlight spills through evening prose.

An old wise owl could not resist,
"Why did the chicken? Oh, I insist!"
He's the punchline master, you can't miss,
Holding court in a feathery twist.

In this landscape where laughter's found,
The echoes rise and dance around.
With every joke, joy's unbound,
In nature's giggles, forever sound!

Inked Stories in the Twisting Vines

In the nooks where the wild vines curl,
A ladybug spins and does a twirl.
"Do you want to dance?" she gives a whirl,
As giggles spread, and petals unfurl.

A chatty parrot drops in quite bold,
With jokes that never get old.
He squawks about treasures untold,
While the garden's laughter starts to unfold.

Among the ferns, a snail recites,
Comedic tales from starry nights.
"My shell is my house, and it's outta sight!"
His punchlines shine like city lights.

Through twisting vines where stories blend,
Laughter weaves and doesn't end.
In this haven, joy's a friend,
A place where giggles always mend!

Beneath the Canopy's Soul

Under leaves, a squirrel slides,
Chasing dreams where acorns hide.
He trips and tumbles in a whirl,
While birds above just chortle and twirl.

The wise old owl gives a chuckle,
As rabbits plan their next big shuffle.
A raccoon shows off his grand ballet,
While fireflies dance to end the day.

Each giggle echoes through the boughs,
As nature wears its laughter's crown.
With every rustle, whispers flow,
Beneath the sky, their joy will grow.

In golden light, the stories flow,
Of critters caught in silly show.
With every chuckle shared in glee,
The forest sings a joyful spree.

Flickers of Life beneath High Branches.

The cheeky chipmunk plays hide and seek,
In the shade, where shadows sneak.
With acorns stacked, he feels so grand,
But slips and falls on the soft, cool land.

A bluebird sings a silly tune,
As ants march by, quite out of tune.
With tiny puffs, they pull their load,
Claiming victory down the road.

The sunbeams play like kids at play,
Creating sprinkles of bright ballet.
Giggling leaves sway in unison,
While critters join the fun they've spun.

Each rustle brings a tale anew,
Laughter spreads like morning dew.
A chorus rises from the ground,
In this happy, lively playground.

Whispers of the Canopy

Beneath the limbs, a secret throng,
Where laughter flows, and nothing's wrong.
A hedgehog dons a tiny hat,
While frogs give jigs, all squishy and fat.

In the shadows, shadows dance,
As fireflies twinkle, lost in chance.
A sly old fox tells a tall tale,
Of journeys made on a tiny scale.

The breeze delivers a comical tune,
As critters laugh beneath the moon.
With every giggle, the night ignites,
Such joy rises with the silver lights.

From roots to tips, the whispers spread,
With each funny story, hearts are fed.
In this realm, mischief runs free,
O, the woodland's merry decree!

Secrets Beneath the Branches

In a grove where whispers twine,
A playful fox steals from the line.
An old raccoon with a snack in paw,
Hides behind bark with a feigned guffaw.

The owls plot mischief in the night,
As squirrels boast of their acorn might.
Among the roots, they bark and tease,
In this forest, laughter's the ultimate breeze.

Hedgehogs skateboard down leafy lanes,
While frogs on lily pads spin in chains.
With every hop, a giggle arises,
In this playhouse, where joy surprises.

So gather round, let stories flow,
Of such funny friends who steal the show.
A chorus sung by creatures small,
In the greenery's arms, we find it all.

Sagas of the Whispering Willows

In the shade where the willows sway,
The squirrels dance and the rabbits play.
They gossip low, their secrets abound,
While birds crack jokes that echo around.

A frog in the pond croaks witty quips,
While fireflies share their light with flips.
The breeze carries laughter, so sweet and clear,
In this lively spot, who needs a beer?

Old raccoon tells of the moon's sly grin,
As the leaves shimmy, and the fun begins.
With shadows casting a playful cloak,
Each sound a chuckle, each whisper a joke.

So gather 'round in this leafy hall,
Where laughter in nature's the best of all.
By the willows, joy sings a tune,
Under the watch of the wise old moon.

Spirit of the Ancient Grove

In the grove where the ancients sigh,
The owls hoot with a twinkle in their eye.
Each rustling leaf has a punchline to share,
As even the bushes join in the flair.

A fox in a waistcoat struts with pride,
While shadows of trees play hide and slide.
A turtle recites poetry slow and grand,
As crickets respond with a tap on the band.

Beneath the branches, secrets unfold,
Like fruit on the vine, stories are told.
The trees chuckle soft, their trunks made of smiles,
While beetles break out in dance for a while.

The spirit of mirth in this magical place,
Whirls 'round the trunks in a light-hearted race.
So join in the fun, let your worries depart,
For joy in the grove is the best kind of art.

The Melodies of Mysterious Meadows

In meadows vast, where daisies spin,
The daisies gossip 'bout things they've seen.
The grasshoppers hop and play the flute,
While butterflies twirl in their fanciest suit.

An ant with a top hat starts a parade,
As flowers sway to the tunes that they made.
A rabbit in shades plays the tambourine,
While bees buzz along, feeling quite keen.

Beneath the blue sky, laughter does bloom,
As the sun draws a smile on every flower's plume.
Each twinkle of dew holds a giggle inside,
In this happy meadow, there's no need to hide.

With stories in petals and secrets in grass,
Nature joins in for a laugh that will last.
So dance in the meadow, let worries all flee,
For joy in the wild is as wild as can be.

Ancestral Echoes in Nature's Chamber

In nature's chamber, echoes are clear,
As the Moonlight Mouse shares tales of cheer.
With wisdom in twinkles, the stars overhear,
And giggles emerge from the forest near.

A spider spins tales with silken style,
While owls roll their eyes with a wise old smile.
Each stone has a story that tickles the ear,
In this grand hall, there's nothing to fear.

Old trees wear their bark like a jester's crown,
And mushrooms crack jokes, never wearing a frown.
As shadows dance lightly with snickers and glee,
The laughter of nature flows wild and free.

So gather the whispers and listen with care,
In this chamber of joy, there's magic to share.
With echoes of laughter that linger and spin,
Nature's the jest, and the fun will begin.

Ephemerals in the Evergreen Dreams

Beneath the giant firs we play,
Where shadows dance, night turns to day.
A squirrel slips, and off he goes,
With acorns tight in tiny toes.

We giggle at the chattering crows,
Who share their secrets, who really knows?
They squawk and flap, what a ruckus!
While we trade laughs, just us and us.

In the dappled light, we spin around,
Avoiding roots that dare to ground.
The pines above chuckle in glee,
At the frolics of hearts so free.

Under this vault of leafy green,
Our laughter echoes, pure and keen.
With whispers from the rustling leaves,
We weave our joys like spider weaves.

Flickering Shadows in the Glade

In the glade where shadows play,
A rabbit hops, then darts away.
The fireflies twinkle, wiggle, and sway,
As moonlight drips like molten clay.

We spot a frog in a silly pose,
So bold he sits, in muddy prose.
With bulging eyes, he croaks a song,
That has us laughing all night long.

The owls up high, in their cunning lair,
Offer wisecracks that hang in the air.
A lizard with flair joins in the jest,
And claims to attend the funniest fest.

Together we sizzle, simmer, and stew,
In laughter's grip, the nighttime crew.
With stories spun in the amber glow,
We share our dreams, both high and low.

Bonds Between Bark and Beneath

The roots tickle as they delve deep,
While branches sway and softly creep.
A friendship blooms where none was sought,
Between the bark and things that rot.

The witty worms, they twist and tease,
As they munch leaves with silly ease.
A wise old oak shakes his head,
At jokes only nature could have said.

A beaver grins with a toothy smile,
Claiming he'll build, just wait a while.
He tries to juggle sticks and stones,
But ups and downs lead to funny groans.

And as we laugh at this leafy mess,
We find ourselves in nature's dress.
With giggles echoing through the land,
We forge our bonds, hand in hand.

In the Embrace of Ancient Pines

In ancient woods so wise and grand,
The gnarled trunks tell tales unplanned.
An acorn drops with a thundering thud,
Sending a startled critter to the mud.

The dance of leaves brings merry cheer,
As squirrels chat, lending an ear.
The pines chuckle, rustling their hair,
While critters gossip without a care.

A humorist frog, in his polka dot-vest,
Claims he's a prince, stands up to jest.
With hops and leaps, he steals the show,
Leaving us all in a fit of woe.

So here we gather, beneath leafy skies,
Where laughter mingles and joy never dies.
In nature's arms, we share our dreams,
Under the gaze of ancient beams.

The Arboreal Archives of Old

Once a squirrel wore a tie,
He claimed he was a spy.
With acorns stashed in his coat,
He'd sneak around, someone wrote.

A wise old owl with glasses round,
Critiqued this squirrel, made quite a sound.
"What's all this fuss? You think you're sly?"
"Just eat your seeds and don't ask why!"

Rabbits gathered, rolling in the grass,
Telling jokes as time would pass.
"Why did the chicken cross the field?"
"To plant a joke that fate revealed!"

Under branches thick and stout,
Laughter echoed, there's no doubt.
For in this realm of merry jest,
Nature's humor stands the test.

Songs from the Shade of Giants

Beneath the limbs of ancient trees,
A raccoon laughed, "I'll tell you, please!"
"Why don't trees ever play hide and seek?"
"Because they always get too weak!"

A fox chimed in, with a clever grin,
"But wait, what about the grapevine kin?"
"They gossip so much, they're never still!"
"Like they've taken a codeine pill!"

Woodpeckers danced, drumming away,
In rhythm with the games we play.
A turtle boasted, slow but wise,
"I've seen more than you with my narrow eyes!"

So gather round and join the spree,
Where stories live, forever free.
In shadows deep, the pranks unfold,
Where every giggle is worth more than gold.

The Allure of the Leafy Tellers

A chipmunk bragged, full of flair,
"I've got the best jokes if you dare!"
"Why did the leaf start to dance?"
"To impress the breeze, it took a chance!"

With a nod, the magpie took a wing,
"That's not half bad, let me bring!"
"Why's the tree always so calm and cool?"
"Because it knows it's no one's fool!"

Caterpillars knit, purling their yarn,
While giggling at the tales they'd garn.
"Do you know what the bark said today?"
"Just let it go, it's all child's play!"

In angles bright where sunlight glows,
The birds take turns with silly prose.
For laughter rings, a joyous sound,
In the company of friends around.

Legends of the Whispering Woods

Where shadows dance, and branches sway,
A hedgehog shouted, "Let's play!"
"Why don't we ever run too fast?"
"Because we might bump into the past!"

The fireflies chimed with flickering light,
"What's more fun, day or night?"
"At night, the stories just are grand!"
"With moonlight as our fairy band!"

A bumblebee buzzed, all around,
"I've got the best buzz, hear my sound!"
"Knock, knock! Who's there, bees?"
"Honeydew! Let's have some teas!"

In these woods where laughters bloom,
Giggles brush away all gloom.
For every whisper brings a cheer,
Memories spun, forever dear.

Enchantment Amidst the Oak Leaves

A squirrel danced on branches high,
Wearing acorns as a hat, oh my!
He twirled and leaped from limb to limb,
While birds joined in, their voices a hymn.

Down below, a rabbit pranced,
With little feet that seemed to dance.
He winked at shadows, played with light,
While frogs croaked loudly, what a sight!

The breeze chuckled through the grove,
As leaves whispered secrets they wove.
The sun peeked in, a cheeky spy,
Making the old tree blush up high.

And when the moon began to rise,
The critters shared their wild surprise.
Each laugh echoed through the night,
As magic sparked 'neath starlit light.

Gentle Murmurs from the Tree Trunks

The wise old elm began to hum,
As bunnies bounced and called, "Come, come!"
They gathered round with hearts aglow,
To hear the tales that breezes blow.

A tiny owl, with glasses cracked,
Said, "I'll share stories, fact by fact!"
With winks and blinks, he'd spin a yarn,
Of moonlight adventures in a barn.

The squirrels clapped, their tails a-fluff,
Giggling 'bout when they'd been tough.
But each mishap brought loud delight,
As laughter echoed into the night.

The trees all leaned, their limbs entwined,
Each trunk a friend, their roots aligned.
In the forest, joy never ends,
For every breeze brings new amends.

Call of the Wildwood

A raccoon strolled with style and flair,
Wearing a jacket, a fine affair.
He tipped his hat to all he met,
While giggling softly, not a fret.

A deer with glasses, reading maps,
Took a wrong turn, fell into laps!
With laughter booming, they straightened up,
And shared a snack from an old wooden cup.

The wind, a jester, played with sound,
Tickled the branches all around.
Each leaf was laughing as squirrels raced,
In this wildwood, humor's embraced.

So if you wander where shadows play,
You'll find the forest's funny display.
With every rustle, there's fun to see,
In nature's realm, wild and free!

Hushed Secrets Among the Saplings

The little saplings gossip and chat,
About the day's events, imagine that!
They whisper low as breezes play,
With tales of wanderers that pass their way.

One sprout claimed it saw a fox,
Wearing bright yellow polka dot socks!
While another laughed till roots turned red,
As visions of giant ants danced in its head.

Frogs leaped in for comedic flair,
Croaking tunes without a care.
The blossoms giggled, petals all aglow,
As whimsy painted the garden's show.

Each night, the stars would join in too,
Glistening above with a playful view.
Among the saplings, laughter takes flight,
In this green theatre, pure delight.

www.ingramcontent.com/pod-product-compliance
Lightning Source LLC
Chambersburg PA
CBHW071851160426
43209CB00003B/510